Habitats
in Need of Help

by Jane St. John

PEARSON
Scott
Foresman

Editorial Offices: Glenview, Illinois • Parsippany, New Jersey • New York, New York
Sales Offices: Needham, Massachusetts • Duluth, Georgia • Glenview, Illinois
Coppell, Texas • Ontario, California • Mesa, Arizona

ISBN: 0-328-13527-5

3 4 5 6 7 8 9 10 V0G1 14 13 12 11 10 09 08 07 06

Habitats as Homes

What is a habitat? It is an **environment** in which a living thing, such as an animal, grows and thrives. Every animal has special requirements of its environment. An animal's habitat must contain enough food, water, shelter, and nesting places for it to survive. A habitat is its home.

Habitats are found all over the world. Your own backyard is a habitat. Oceans, rivers, and freshwater lakes are water habitats. Forests, deserts, and prairies are land habitats. Habitats are all around us, and some of them are at risk.

Natural disasters can destroy peoples' homes and animals' habitats.

What would you do if your home was destroyed? Families who survive natural disasters, such as tornadoes and hurricanes, sometimes face this question. Fortunately, it is only rarely that people lose their homes due to natural disasters. For animals, however, habitat loss occurs much more often. Nature sometimes destroys animals' habitats. A beaver's dam can be ruined in a rainstorm, and a sudden snowstorm can wreck a bird's nest.

Scientists called ecologists have found that increasing human populations and their daily activities directly **contribute** to the loss of many animal habitats. Today, about 50 percent of the world's land surface is considered destroyed or disturbed. By 2032 that level may reach 70 percent. Destruction of animal habitats threatens to ruin entire ecosystems, or environments, and the animals that live in them. We must discover and learn about new ways to protect these ecosystems.

Land at Risk

The black bear is one animal whose habitat has been deeply impacted by humans. Black bears like to live in old forests filled with hardwood trees. In spring and summer they feed on the forest's berries and leaves. In the fall they remain deep in the woods, where the plant growth is thick, as they prepare to hibernate for the winter.

Black bears are shy by nature and avoid humans. Many of their habitats, however, have been destroyed due to the construction of houses and roads. In many regions, bears have had to learn to become more comfortable around humans in order to survive.

Near Lake Tahoe, California, black bears discovered that they could feed and rest comfortably in an environment controlled by humans. Now, the black bears of Lake Tahoe feed on scraps of food from garbage cans and campsites and sleep under people's porches.

Black bears' lives have changed dramatically in places where humans have altered their habitats.

The black bears of Yosemite National Park have learned that it is easier to find scraps of food in the cars and trash of the park's visitors than it is to wander around looking for berries.

Park officials have developed regulations to help visitors avoid contact with bears. These regulations warn visitors to hide their food. Without these regulations, bears would continue to depend on humans for food instead of relying on their natural environment. Sometimes, a black bear becomes so dependent on humans that park officials are forced to move the bear to another part of the park.

Some black bears are too dependent on humans for food.

Habitat destruction has caused orangutan populations to decline.

Another forest-dwelling animal whose habitat is at risk is the orangutan. Its homes are the island of Borneo and the neighboring Indonesian island of Sumatra. This huge ape (ranging from sixty to three hundred pounds) needs large areas of forest in which to roam. Unfortunately, humans have taken over land for mining, logging, and various types of farming, so less than 20 percent of the orangutan's original habitat remains.

When a habitat is destroyed, the animal's food supply decreases, and it can no longer thrive. During the past one hundred years, orangutan populations have decreased by about 90 percent. Some researchers estimate that there are fewer than thirty thousand orangutans on the islands today.

Many organizations are concerned about the survival of orangutans. Orangutan Foundation International is one group working to protect the tropical forests that orangutans call home.

Like orangutans, Asian elephants are threatened by habitat loss. Asian elephants live on forest-covered lands. But those lands are also used by 1.5 billion people, leading to an uneasy mix. In India, Thailand, and Sumatra, the clearing of forests–in many cases to make space for growing human populations–has placed Asian elephants in serious trouble.

Forest clearing has resulted in a loss of Asian elephants' natural habitat. This loss is especially troubling for Asian elephants because they are migratory. Now, when Asian elephants migrate, they become trapped in small forest pockets.

Just as groups are working to save the habitats of orangutans, others are working to protect forests that elephants call home.

Like their Asian cousins, African elephants are threatened by habitat loss.

Monach butterflies are as small as Asian elephants are large. But as with Asian elephants, human activities have severely affected their migration patterns. Migrating monarch butterflies fly from North America to Mexico for the winter. There they rest before returning north for the summer. Part of Mexico's evergreen forest is a protective shelter for the butterfly.

In spite of this, the forested region is losing trees at an alarming rate. Once the tourists and butterflies have left for the season, loggers come to clear the land. In Mexico there is an increasing demand for wood and the crops that can be planted on cleared land.

Habitat loss in Mexican forests has caused major problems for the monarch butterfly.

Growth in farming has hurt natural habitats.

Unfortunately, Mexico is not the only country where the clearing of land for crops has hurt habitats. There are many examples of habitats that have been damaged or destroyed to make room for farmland. In the United States alone, more than 90 percent of our native prairies have been lost to farms.

Changing habits and demands of humans can forever change an ecosystem. For example, worldwide demand for rice, wheat, and corn is expected to grow 40 percent by 2020. This means that the demand for irrigation—changing the paths of waterways to get water to crops—is expected to rise 50 percent or more. In all likelihood this will lead to increased pressure to transform many areas into agricultural regions.

Scientists have identified approximately fifty "dead zones" along the world's coasts, where ocean creatures can no longer live.

Water Habitats in Danger

Land habitats are not the only ones in danger. Marine habitats, and the animals that live in them, are threatened as well. There are about fifty "dead zones" along the world's coasts, for example. These are areas in which those coastlines' ocean creatures simply can no longer live. The largest dead zone in the Western Hemisphere is along the Gulf of Mexico. There, excess phosphorus and nitrogen from the Mississippi River flowed into the Gulf and damaged the ecosystem.

A specific example of the harm caused by dead zones involves the Mexican gray whale. In 1999, dozens of gray whales were reported killed off the coast of Mexico. It was suspected that they had died from excess salt in the water. The salt had come from salt-making operations near the coast.

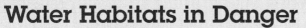

Mexican gray whale

Of all the whale species that swim the coast of the United States, the humpback whale is probably the most famous. Its fame comes from the dazzling leaps and displays that it makes. Today, there are perhaps ten thousand humpbacks worldwide. This is estimated to be 8 percent of the original humpback whale population. In the mid-1800s, about 125,000 humpback whales lived worldwide. Like other whales, they were hunted for their meat, oil, and a substance called baleen attached to their jaws. At that time, whale oil was used in street lamps, and baleen was used to make women's dresses.

In 1966 the International Whaling Commission gave all humpbacks protected status, by prohibiting people from hunting them. However, some countries have ignored the ban and continue to hunt. Humpbacks have also been hurt by becoming entangled in fishing gear and ocean debris. Ship collisions have resulted in humpback whales being stranded, and jet skis and parasails near Hawaii have been hazardous to humpbacks and their ecosystem.

The overeating of sea otters by orcas led to the reduction of kelp forests in Alaskan coastal waters.

The hunting of whales can have a domino effect on other species as well, as an **investigation** into changes in Alaska's coastal ecosystems revealed. Off the coast of Alaska, from the 1940s through the 1970s, overfishing of many of the species of large whales, such as fins and humpbacks, caused orcas to seek prey other than the large whales that they normally ate. Orcas began to prey on harbor seals, then fur seals, then sea lions, and, at last, sea otters for food. The sea otter population was reduced to such a low level that there were not enough of them to feed on all the sea urchins. This caused the sea urchin population to grow by a huge amount. Sea urchins overgrazed, which led to the reduction of Alaska's kelp forests in its coastal waters.

Coral reefs are one kind of ocean habitat. Like kelp forests, they have experienced trouble. In fact, coral reefs are considered endangered. A reef is a fragile limestone framework in which corals and other types of animals, such as jellyfish, sea urchins, and sponges, live. It is believed that up to 25 percent of the world's coral reefs have already been destroyed. Overfishing, marine pollution, and an increase in viral and bacterial diseases that can kill coral are to blame.

Tropical storms, such as cyclones and hurricanes, make reefs weaker and more prone to habitat destruction. Reefs have also been affected by human activities. Australia's Great Barrier Reef is one such reef. Its population of nesting loggerhead turtles has decreased greatly since the 1960s. It is believed that this can be directly traced to increased farming and material deposited in the ocean through runoff.

Many other species of marine life in the world's oceans are also in trouble. For example, it is estimated that since the 1950s tuna and marlin populations have been reduced by 90 percent, due to overfishing and harmful fishing methods.

Overfishing has been so harmful that, even when fishing has been reduced, it has taken several years for the fish to "catch up." For example, Canada and New England's cod populations dropped so low in the 1990s that only 1 percent of their original population remained. The Canadian government closed cod fishing areas for several years to allow the species to recover. Still, the cod population remains very low.

Red snapper, which lives off the west coast of the United States, is another fish that is now in danger. Overfishing is to blame, along with the fact that shrimp trawlers often capture 10 to 20 million very young red snappers every year.

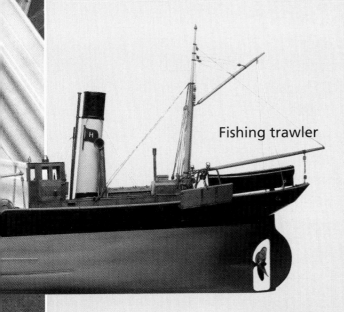

Fishing trawler

The polar bear is the largest of the eight bear species on Earth. It lives along the Arctic Circle, in North America, Russia, and Norway. The polar bear is considered the world's largest land predator. It is the only bear that eats mostly meat. But today polar bears are under pressure. The gradual warming of their habitat has caused ice packs to break up across the Arctic.

The melting of the polar ice caps means the bears are often stranded onshore and have less time to fatten up each summer. As a result, some female bears cannot produce enough milk for their cubs, and fewer cubs are able to survive the harsh winters. Polar bears are also threatened by oil spills. Oil partially strips the polar bear's fur of its warming properties and covers the bear's prey as well. Toxic chemicals and air pollution also threaten the Arctic region.

Air Troubles

The air quality of an environment can affect habitats too. In parts of Inner Mongolia, mining activities and accidents have sparked numerous fires in underground coal mines. The fires have put harmful chemicals into the air. These chemicals have polluted the groundwater that animals drink and produced acid rain that destroys the plants that some animals eat.

Although Inner Mongolia probably has the worst problem with coal fires, they have also occured in India, Indonesia, and even the United States. In 1962 an abandoned mine in Centralia, Pennsylvania, was used to burn trash. The fire from the burning trash grew out of control. As a result, the fire is still burning, and has caused devastation and destruction of many habitats.

Wind turbines such as these are a great source for clean energy, but they have led to the deaths of many birds.

Wind turbines, in contrast to coal, are a source of clean, renewable energy. Unlike power plants, they do not pollute while generating electricity. Unfortunately, despite these benefits, the wind turbines on modern wind farms have killed many birds. Near San Francisco, California, it is estimated that 22,000 birds have been killed by the blades on wind turbines. The wind turbines have only been around for a couple of decades. Because of that, California's birds have not yet learned to change their flight paths, thereby avoiding the turbines. One suggestion that people have made to help birds adjust is to paint the blades of the wind turbines in colors and patterns that birds can see more easily. This might encourage the birds to fly farther away from the machines.

Factories and power plants are a major cause for habitat loss and destruction.

Helping Habitats

You have just read about many habitats and ecosystems that are in danger. Habitats can be spoiled in two main ways. Either the amount of habitat is reduced, such as when a wetland is paved for a highway, or the quality of the habitat is changed. A company that dumps toxic wastes into a waterway is reducing the quality of that ecosystem.

In 1995 the United States Geological Survey documented the extent to which habitats in our country were in danger. Altogether it listed 126 ecosystems as being either critically endangered, endangered, or threatened.

Technological improvements, while mostly positive, also have the unfortunate side effect of causing large-scale damage to happen more quickly than it did in the past. But what can we do to halt and repair this damage?

Fortunately, there are many successful examples of states, organizations, and individuals working to preserve habitats. For example, the states of Delaware and Virginia have programs that encourage citizens to understand ecological resources. West Virginia allows its residents to adopt birds at its Raptor Rehabilitation Center. South Dakota is a leader in preserving prairie lands. A **conservation** program there has encouraged ranchers to return farmland to native grassland while still allowing cows and other animals to graze.

You, too, can help in many ways. Visit your local library or historical society to see some before-and-after photographs of development in your area to understand how the habitat around you has changed. Be an **enthusiastic** supporter of efforts to save local habitats and the animals that live in them. Talk to your family. Put your habitat-saving ideas into action!

Glossary

conservation *n.* preservation from harm or decay.

contribute *v.* to help bring about.

enthusiastic *adj.* full of enthusiasm; eagerly interested.

environment *n.* the circumstances or conditions of air, water, and soil.

investigation *n.* a careful search.